SPORTS HEROES

CARMELO ANTHONY

Sloan MacRae

PowerKiDS press™

New York

Published in 2012 by The Rosen Publishing Group, Inc.
29 East 21st Street, New York, NY 10010

First Edition

Editor: Jennifer Way
Book Design: Julio Gil

Photo Credits: Cover Chris Trotman/Getty Images; cover (background) Jarrett Baker/Getty Images; p. 5 Mike Ehrmann/Getty Images; p. 6 Sporting News/Sporting News via Getty Images; pp. 7 (left, right), 13 Jed Jacobsohn/Getty Images; pp. 8–9 Manny Millan/Sports Illustrated/Getty Images; pp. 10, 11 (left) Craig Jones/Getty Images; p. 11 (right) Al Bello/Getty Images; p. 12 Andy Lyons/Getty Images; pp. 14–15 Brian Bahr/Getty Images; p. 16 Bob Rosato/Sports Illustrated/Getty Images; pp. 17, 18, 19 Nick Laham/Getty Images; p. 20 Garrett W. Ellwood/NBAE via Getty Images; p. 21 James Devaney/WireImage/Getty Images; p. 22 Ronald Martinez/Getty Images.

Library of Congress Cataloging-in-Publication Data

MacRae, Sloan.
 Carmelo Anthony / by Sloan MacRae. — 1st ed.
    p. cm. — (Sports heroes)
 Includes index.
 ISBN 978-1-4488-6160-6 (library binding) — ISBN 978-1-4488-6278-8 (pbk.) —
ISBN 978-1-4488-6279-5 (6-pack)
 1. Anthony, Carmelo, 1984-—Juvenile literature. 2. Basketball players—United States—Biography—Juvenile literature. I. Title.
 GV884.A58M34 2012
 796.323092—dc23
 [B]
                          2011019527

Manufactured in the United States of America

CPSIA Compliance Information: Batch #WW12PK: For Further Information contact Rosen Publishing, New York, New York at 1-800-237-9932

★ CONTENTS

MELO

Some sports stars take a long time to become great. They practice for years before they finally get a chance to prove themselves. Carmelo Anthony found success early, though. He joined the National Basketball Association, or NBA, when he was only 19 years old!

Carmelo Anthony is known for his ability to score lots of points in a game. In 2008, he tied an NBA record when he scored 33 points in one quarter!

Anthony has quickly become one of the best **professional** basketball players of all time. He has also become one of the most popular because he is so fun to watch. Many fans simply call him Melo. Melo is a **small forward** for the New York Knicks and will be one of the sports world's hottest stars for many years to come.

FROM BROOKLYN TO BALTIMORE

Here is Carmelo with his mother, Mary, after his college basketball team, the Syracuse Orange, won the NCAA championship in 2003. >>>

Carmelo was born in a **borough** of New York City called Brooklyn in a **neighborhood** called Red Hook. Growing up, Carmelo had four siblings. He had a sad childhood. His father died when Carmelo was only two years old. When Carmelo was eight, his family moved to Baltimore, Maryland. Crime and drugs are big problems in some parts of Baltimore. These neighborhoods are not

>>> Anthony (right) has played in the NBA All-Star Game four times since becoming a professional player. The NBA's best players are picked to take part in this game.

very safe. This was true of the poor neighborhood where Carmelo grew up. Carmelo loved basketball, and he became very good at it. Because he worked so hard and spent so much time practicing, basketball kept Carmelo out of trouble.

Here is Anthony during the 2010 All-Star Game. ❯❯❯

HIGH-SCHOOL HOOPS

It did not always seem as though Carmelo would become a great basketball player. In fact, he did not even make the Towson Catholic High School basketball team the first time he tried out!

Here is Carmelo in 2002, playing in the McDonald's All-American Game. This is a game played by the best high-school basketball players in the United States and Canada.

Carmelo worked hard over the summer and joined the team his **sophomore**, or second, year. Basketball fans in Baltimore started paying attention to this great young player. Carmelo struggled in school, though. There was a chance that his grades would not be good enough to get him into a good college. He moved to a new high school, called Oak Hill Academy in Virginia. He brought his grades up, and he also became one of the best young **athletes** in the country.

AT SYRACUSE

Anthony was named 2003's NCAA Men's Basketball Tournament Most Outstanding Player because of how well he played during the championship.

Carmelo decided to go to college at Syracuse University, in New York. Syracuse has one of the most famous basketball programs in the United States. At Syracuse, Anthony found a great **mentor** in his coach, Jim Boeheim. The two worked well together, and Anthony's basketball career got off to a better start than anyone could have imagined. Every year the best college basketball teams **compete** in the NCAA Division I Basketball

Shortly after winning the 2003 NCAA tournament, Anthony got to take part in an NCAA tradition. After winning the final game, each player on the winning team cuts down a piece of the net.

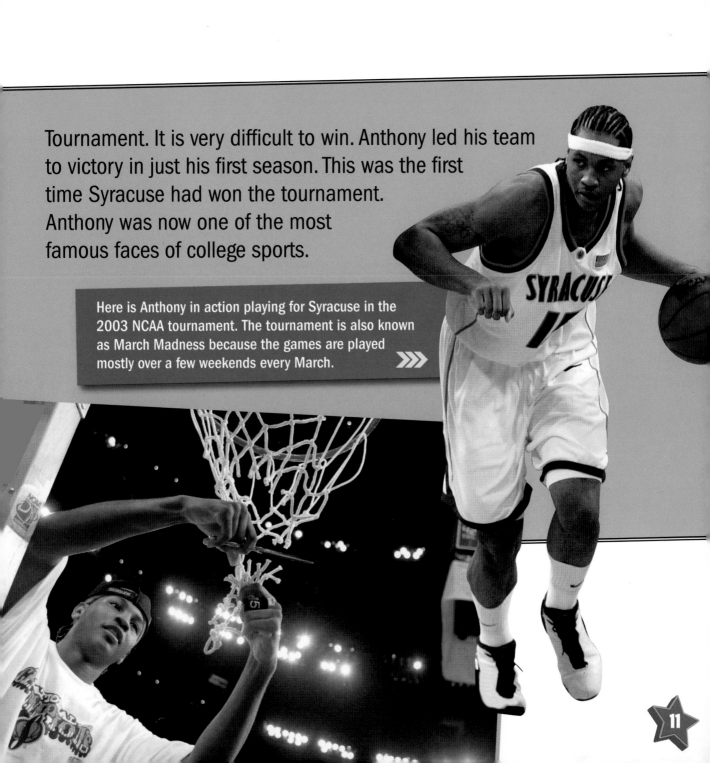

Tournament. It is very difficult to win. Anthony led his team to victory in just his first season. This was the first time Syracuse had won the tournament. Anthony was now one of the most famous faces of college sports.

Here is Anthony in action playing for Syracuse in the 2003 NCAA tournament. The tournament is also known as March Madness because the games are played mostly over a few weekends every March.

Anthony decided to leave Syracuse after his freshman, or first, year. Syracuse had just won the NCAA tournament and Anthony had been named the tournament's Most Outstanding Player. Anthony's abilities were becoming well known to basketball fans and professional basketball coaches. After talking with Syracuse coach

Anthony was chosen for the 2003–2004 NBA All-Rookie Team. This is a yearly honor that goes to the best new players in the NBA. »»

Jim Boeheim, Anthony decided to leave Syracuse and go to the NBA.

Only the best basketball players in the world compete in the NBA. The Denver Nuggets picked Anthony in the 2003 NBA **Draft**. The Nuggets hoped this great young player could help them turn things around. At the time, they were one of the worst teams in basketball.

««« LeBron James (right) was another young player chosen for the 2003–2004 NBA All-Rookie Team.

The Denver Nuggets finished with a 17 and 65 record in the year before Anthony joined the team. This means that they won only 17 games all season! Many fans stopped buying tickets. The Nuggets hoped that Anthony would help the team win more games and get fans excited about the Nuggets again.

After being chosen to play in the All-Star Game in 2007, Anthony was picked again in 2008, 2010, and 2011. Here Anthony is playing with the Nuggets against the Los Angeles Lakers.

Anthony had a great **rookie** season. In Anthony's first professional season, he helped the Denver Nuggets reach the NBA **playoffs**. Anthony only got better over the next few years, and so did the Nuggets. Anthony played in his first All-Star Game in 2007. Only the biggest stars in the NBA get to play in this game.

15

Many young athletes dream of representing their country in the Olympic Games. The United States fields a basketball team to compete in the Summer Games. Anthony got his chance to play for the U.S. team in 2004 in the Olympics in Athens, Greece.

Anthony scored 13 points in the gold-medal game against Spain in the 2008 Olympics. The U.S. team was very proud to bring home the gold medal.

The American team did not play as well as they were expected to, though. They won the bronze medal.

Anthony once again joined the American basketball team in the 2008 Summer Olympics, in Beijing, China. This time the American team played very well. They **defeated** Spain's team and took home the gold medal!

Anthony (center) helped the U.S. basketball team bring home the gold in the 2008 Olympics. Here the U.S. team is playing against Germany.

From 2003 until 2011, Anthony made basketball history playing for the Nuggets. The Nuggets became a much better team and were winning more games. Fans were excited to watch Anthony play. In 2011, other teams hoped Anthony could repeat his success with them.

The New York Knicks were once a great team, but they had had several bad seasons. The Knicks thought they could build a

Anthony (right) helped the Knicks reach the NBA playoffs for the first time since 2000. However, they lost to the Boston Celtics in the first round.

good team around Anthony. They made a deal with the Nuggets, and Anthony joined the Knicks in February 2011. He helped his new team get their first winning season since 2000. Anthony also helped the Knicks reach the playoffs. Denver fans were sad to see him go, but New York fans could not be happier to have him on their team!

Here is Anthony soon after he joined the Knicks. The other Nuggets players who were traded to the Knicks then along with Anthony were Chauncey Billups, Shelden Williams, Anthony Carter, and Renaldo Balkman.

Family is very important to Anthony. He knows that his mother, Mary, worked hard to help him make his dreams come true. Carmelo wants to do the same for his child. He is married to La La Vazquez. They have a son named Kiyan, who was born in 2007.

Here is Carmelo with his wife, La La, and their son, Kiyan. »»

When Anthony is not playing basketball, he works to help others. He never forgot where he came from. Anthony gave millions of dollars to Syracuse to create a basketball center. He also works to help poor children in Baltimore succeed in school and stay out of trouble.

««« Anthony knows how important school and sports are in keeping kids out of trouble. That is why he likes doing charity work that keeps kids focused on school and school sports.

FUN FACTS

>>> Anthony broke the record for points scored by a freshman in the NCAA tournament with 33 points in a game against the University of Texas.

>>> He became the second-youngest player in NBA history to score 5,000 points.

>>> One of Anthony's best friends is the great basketball star LeBron James.

>>> Anthony has a dog named Stoney. It is a Shar-Pei.

>>> Since he grew up in Baltimore, Anthony is a fan of the Ravens and the Orioles.

>>> Anthony opened a barbershop in Denver that gives free haircuts to poor children.

>>> Anthony owns a company called Krossover Entertainment that records music.

>>> Anthony threw a Christmas party called A Very Melo Christmas to help poor children in Denver.

>>> Anthony produces a TV show that stars his wife, La La.

>>> Carmelo Anthony has appeared on several television shows, including *Saturday Night Live*, the *Late Show with David Letterman*, and *Conan*.

GLOSSARY

athletes (ATH-leets) People who take part in sports.

borough (BUR-oh) In New York City, one of five parts into which the city is divided.

compete (kum-PEET) To oppose another in a game or contest.

defeated (dih-FEET-ed) To have beat another in a game.

draft (DRAFT) The selection of people for a special purpose.

mentor (MEN-tor) A trusted guide or teacher.

neighborhood (NAY-ber-hud) A place where people live together.

playoffs (PLAY-ofs) Games played after the regular season ends to see who will play in the championship.

professional (pruh-FESH-nul) Someone who is paid for what he or she does.

rookie (RU-kee) A new major-league player.

small forward (SMAWL FOR-werd) A basketball player who is expected to score a lot of points and play good defense.

sophomore (SOF-mor) A student in his or her second year of high school or college.

INDEX

Due to the changing nature of Internet links, PowerKids Press has developed an online list of Web sites related to the subject of this book. This site is updated regularly. Please use this link to access the list:
www.powerkidslinks.com/hero/anthony/